The Next Thing Always Belongs

The Next Thing Always Belongs

POEMS

Chris Anderson

Airlie
Press

Airlie Press is supported by book sales and subscription orders,
by contributions to the press from its supporters,
and by the work donated by all the poet-editors of the press.

Major funding has been provided by:
Sara J. Burant & Eugene D. Johnson
Julia Wills
and the friends and supporters
of Airlie Press

Cover art: *Place* by Denise Ross
Author photo: Nancy Froehlich
Design: Cheryl McLean

PO Box 434
Monmouth, OR 97361
airliepress@yahoo.com
www.airliepress.org

ISBN 978-0-9821066-5-5
Library of Congress Control Number: 2011926070

Printed in the United States of America

in memory of my mother

In a sense, the next thing always belongs.
—Richard Hugo

Acknowledgments

Grateful acknowledgment is made to the editors of the publications where these poems or earlier versions of these poems first appeared:

"The Rosary Confuses My Dogs" and "Limited Edition,"
   The Eloquent Umbrella

"A Summer Day," "Wisdom," and "Why I Like the
   Tomb," *Spiritus*

"The Other Side," "Move Over, Darling," and "The
   Junco and the Boy," *Rattle*

"Password," *The Cortland Review*

"Lucy," "But My, Don't the Trees Seem Full," "Stardust,"
   and "Everything That Rises Must Converge," *The
   Apple Valley Review*

"People of Galilee" and "Neighbors," *Pilgrimage*

"Birds I Have Known," *Windfall*

"Plow," *32 Poems*

"River of Light," *Stringtown*

"Sliver," *High Desert Journal*

"Bing Crosby's Dorm," *Cold Mountain Review*

"I Tell Mr. Rogers My Dog Died," *Rosebud*

"Hank Asks about Angels" and "Whatever Else, the
   Blessed Days," *Poetry East*

"Stephen Hawking Experiences Weightlessness" and
   "We Will Go Rejoicing," *Bellowing Ark*

"Three Theories of the Spine," *Hubbub*

"Seven More Parables of the Kingdom," "Morning with
   the Dying Man," and "What Trees Do," *The Cresset*

"Rose," *Ascent*

In a brief section of notes at the end of the book, I acknowledge some of the sources I draw on in these and other poems—passages from scripture, biographies, jokes, movies, and various lines and phrases from other writers. I also explain a few of the terms I use from my work as a deacon.

My gratitude to the members of my writing group: Eric Dickey, Steve Jones, and especially to Michael Malan, who has had an enormous influence on my writing.

My gratitude to the poets of Airlie Press, for accepting me into the collective and for all their help and support: Donna Henderson, Jessica Lamb, Carter McKenzie, Anita Sullivan, Cecelia Hagen, and Stephanie Lenox. Airlie Press is a remarkable enterprise, and I am honored to be a part of it.

My gratitude to Lex Runciman and Richard Wakefield, for their wise and compassionate counsel.

My gratitude to Catherine Otto, for her remarkably generous reading of the manuscript, and to Madeline Otto, for her insightful comments.

My gratitude to all the people I've come to know in my ministry, for all the stories they've given me to tell. It is a great, great privilege to be able to serve this community.

My gratitude to Piper Jones, for allowing me to share the story of her father.

My gratitude to Denise Ross, for allowing me to use her beautiful photograph for the cover of the book.

My gratitude to Cheryl McLean, for her wonderful design of the cover and of the page.

My gratitude to Roberta Sobotka, for her expert proofreading.

Most of all, my gratitude to Barb.

Contents

I

The Rosary Confuses My Dogs

When, walking in the woods,
I pull out my long black rosary,

parallel between rosary and leash

the beads loop down and jingle
a little like the leash when I pull it out
to put the dogs back on.

And the dogs, when they hear it,
come running up,
heads cocked, tongues lolling.

No, I say. It's OK.
And they bound away again.

God → us   Owner → dog

A Summer Day

A ukulele band strums by the grave
of an old woman I never knew.
I lead the prayers, alb flapping, *(white catholic priest robe)*
helping to lay the body to rest,
and as the family lingers,
quietly walk away, down the hill
to another grave I remember from before.

It was winter then, and the oak was bare,
and the one we buried was a boy.
"I keep thinking he'll be cold,"
the father said. "He'll need his coat."

But it's summer now, and the farmers
are haying in their yellow fields.
The dust of the harvest is softening the air.
And as I stand at the market, looking out,
a feeling starts to come over me,
a kind of peace, almost like the peace
I prayed for up the hill, the peace of God,
which surpasses all understanding.
It spreads through my body like warmth.

(caesura)
I know. I'm just saying what happened.
I'm just saying that it surprised me, too.
The farmers, and the yellow fields,
and the warm, summer wind.
The ukulele band, strumming still.

(handwritten notes:)
- seasons
- enjambment
- strophic → stanzas, yes ✓

4

stichic → no stanzas

The Other Side

The falling of a leaf onto a pond is one movement
in a process composed of many movements.
It floats for a while, crisply. Then softens and sinks.
It's funny what comes to mind. All day I think
about a woman I haven't seen in many years.
Her soft, brown hair. The way the corners of her eyes
pulled down. It's not that I am filled with longing
or regret. But I am filled with something. *Volta*
In a dream I climb a hill on the other side of town.
It is an arduous climb. At the end I am afraid
of falling. But then I look down and realize
all the houses are exactly like the house I live in.
In the distance, the same kind of highway.
Everything is the same. It's just on the other side.

priming

a turning of attention

Lucy

When I lived for a month in a hut by the sea,
back home my little red dog ran away.
I was walking in a cemetery on a hill, looking
at the gravestones, and the thought crossed

my mind: Lucy has run away. And she had,
I found out, that very day, and she didn't come
back for hours. It wasn't an intuition exactly.
It was just a thought. But all those thirty days

I was more porous than usual, more aware
of all the signs that God sends us, or might,
and I often missed Lucy and thought about her.
I kept seeing her face in the faces of the deer

or the chipmunks or even the birds. I was
aware of how everything has a face. That
we have eyes and so do the animals, all of them.
We have ears and so do they. They kept me

company in that long, lonely month trying
to pray and sometimes feeling thinned out,
opened. Sunsets. Clouds coming and going.
Dreams. Once, touching the trunk of a tree.

Since then I've suffered several losses,
and it's been a lot harder to stay on the path
and follow the call than I thought it would be.
Sometimes where we find ourselves

is in the desert. More and more I think
life is about letting things go, or trying to.
It's about giving things up. It's about holding
things in memory and believing in them still.

The night before I gave Lucy away,
I brushed her long red hair until it shone,
combing out the tangles. She leaned against me
as I worked and I kept hugging her and talking

to her. "Oh Lucy," I kept saying, "I have to."
In the morning, when she hopped into his car
and my friend drove her away, she looked
from the back like a beautiful young girl.

Move Over, Darling

I have to admit that sometimes
I don't care about the historical Jesus.
One way or the other.
I've always thought there were other forces at work, too.
The sun and the wind.
The sadness that comes in the late afternoon.
Did you know that our bones are only ten years old?
No matter how old we are, it's always the same.
Something to do with the cells, I guess. With regeneration.
There are miracles like this all over the place,
in everybody's bloodstream, and that's alright with me.
Doris Day was once marooned on an island with another man.
Years went by and her husband, James Garner,
was about to marry another woman. Polly Bergen.
But then Doris came back and sang a lullaby to her kids
and tucked them into bed,
and they didn't even know who she was.
I think life is just like that.
Sometimes we are the rock, and the Spirit is the river.
Sometimes we are the mountain, and the Spirit is the rain.

The Junco and the Boy

Over the weekend I shot a bird. A deranged, obsessive junco
that had been banging against our window for weeks, fluttering
in and up, again and again, hundreds of times a day, enraged
by its own reflection. You can't reason with a bird, and this one
we couldn't scare away, with flags or foil or glittering strips.

Nothing worked. After a while even Barb wanted me to kill it.
We woke up Saturday at five when it started hurling itself
at us again, for another day, and she said, *Get a gun*. So I went
to a friend of mine, our lawyer, a Republican, and he loaned me
a rifle, patiently demonstrating how to load the birdshot

and find the target, and I spent the afternoon stalking through
my own backyard, firing and missing, firing and missing.
It's been forty years since I shot a gun—at scout camp
one summer, at the lake, when I got my shooting merit badge.
We were the sort of parents who never even let our kids

have toy guns, who wouldn't let them make sticks into guns,
even though in the end our oldest son became a soldier
and went to Iraq and is on his way there now a second time,
an expert with an M-16 and the .50-caliber machine gun
they mount on all the gun trucks. My son. I'd never even

been on an army base until we went to Fort Benning to watch
him graduate from infantry training. We sat in the bleachers
like at a football game, and the loudspeakers started blaring
"Bad to the Bone," and then these soldiers came out
of the woods firing blanks at the crowd through an orange

and yellow smoke screen. I was kind of impressed at first,
I have to admit, though Barb just wept. What bothered me
was that we couldn't tell where he was in all the blocks
of marching soldiers, later, on the parade ground, all of them
sheared and pressed and squared, all of them the same. It was

the knob on the back of his head that gave him away, and
even then it was as if he were older somehow, older and younger
at the same time, and in a kind of time warp, too. It was like
we were all somehow trapped inside a World War II movie.
Pearl Harbor had been bombed and we were striking back.

I couldn't shake this feeling. When I finally hit the junco,
on something like my fifteenth try, I think—he had flown into
a magnolia, next to the deck, and maybe it was luck or maybe
I was getting the hang of it again, but I squeezed the trigger
and the rifle fired, and the bird twitched, then dropped,

straight down, into the backyard—when I finally hit it,
I didn't feel guilty exactly. I'm not sure what I felt. I know
I wanted to get rid of that bird. I know how frustrated I was
with the fluttering and the banging. I know how embarrassed
I'd been all afternoon, firing and missing, firing and missing.

Later I drove our four-year-old grandson into town, to the store.
I haven't done this in a long time, either. He's our step-
grandson. The woman John married before he left this weekend
has two little boys. So we have these new, instant grandsons
and I'm still adjusting. But it was good to know that I could

do this still. Strap a little boy into a car seat. Talk to him
on the way, looking into the rearview mirror. Bribe him
and pace him and manage him through the aisles of the store
as we got our cereal and butter and bread. All the way home,
driving through the fields, I had this feeling that the Honda

hardly weighed a thing, it was light as a feather, and so was
that little boy. His small, brown knees. His skinny,
brown arms. Everything was hollow. Everything was light.
I thought, when we get back home and I reach in to get him,
he'll be no trouble at all. I'll be able to lift him with one hand.

People of Galilee

People of Galilee!
Why do you have your heads in the clouds?

Not only is there no God,
try finding a plumber on the weekend.
Ta dah duh.

Once there was a cop in Malta, Montana,
who had a wife named Toots.

She was Indian, a Blackfoot, and she gave my baby brother
a necklace of claws to frighten his asthma away.
Who's to say it didn't work?

Another time we snuck down to the river, the Milk River,
where the older boys would fish.
They'd sit on an old couch and throw out their lines.

We weren't allowed to go there, of course,
but that day we did, and we watched as they pulled
from those silty, glacial waters
a marvelous golden fish, every scale perfectly articulated.

When it spoke, it said, *Rejoice*.

Neighbors

Samuel Beckett used to drive
Andre the Giant to school every day.
They were neighbors in Paris,
Beckett and Andre's family,
and even as a boy, before
he became a famous wrestler,
Andre was too big for the bus.

Beckett may have been
an Absurdist, with his rugged,
handsome face, like a fisherman's.
He may have written "nothing
is funnier than unhappiness."
But in real life he was
a good neighbor. He was kind.

I think this is really something
to consider. It takes
540 million years to evolve
an eyeball, with all its layered
and subtle membranes,
its miraculous dark aperture.
What, then, will we see?

The Watchful Tree

When the Lord came to me
I was looking at a branch of the Watchful Tree.

I was waiting for the kettle to boil.
I was admiring the potter at his wheel.

And the Lord said, Yes, the wheel is turning
and the kettle sings
and the almond tree is the Watchful Tree
because it is the first to bloom in the spring.

We watch for it.

I walk into a room and the woman I meet
seems to give off light.
Something is glowing inside of her,
maybe an emptiness,
and it leaks out the corners of her eyes.

I can see it.

I walk into a room and I sit down by a man
and there is a darkness inside of him, a meanness.

I seem to see a sheet of oil
sliding down a pane of glass.

Hummingbirds bicker by the feeder, buzzing
and brawling and shooting away. Or they hover
there, in their beauty. Impossibly. Shimmering.

The way every season contains the next
and foreshadows it.

The yellow leaves in the summer green.
The shining branch, deep in the heart of the tree.

Sacristan

Always dressed to the nines.
Tweed skirts. Silver hair just so.
Sometimes she'd hiss at me
from the pews, during Mass,
as I was arranging
the cups or placing the book. "No!
To the left! The left!"
When she finally lost her mind,
I went over to the assisted care facility
to bring her Communion,
carrying the consecrated host
in a small, silver pyx.
She welcomed me formally.
"Won't you please sit," she said,
then calmly peeled off her housedress,
up over her head, like a girl—
right there, in front of me—
and stood before her closet, in her slip,
deciding what to wear.
I had brought Christ into that room.
She knew she had to change.

The Old Woman and the Stars

In Sublimity her husband got so drunk
she had to drag him to bed by his boots.

But it wasn't his face she saw.
It was the face of Jesus.

"How deep is your love?" he asked her.

Another night she saw the veil
that covers the world
hanging over their bed like a net.

She reached up and pulled it down
and rubbed it on her hands and arms.
It was soft as cheesecloth.

Water flows over stones.
A breeze blows from the mountains.

The desert isn't such a bad place,
especially in the morning and the evening
when the air is cool and the stars are out.

Did you know this?
There are nine galaxies
for every person alive on earth.

Foundation

Catherine gets down on her hands and knees
and crawls beneath the house. She is helping
her husband shore up the floor. His heart. His hope.
Spelunking, she shouts through the floorboards:

"Nail here!" Or later in the day, still underneath,
she turns to see hundreds of baby spiders
bursting from an egg sac, thousands of them,
skittering over the fine cracks in the foundation.

"This is the way," they say. "Walk in it."

Birds I Have Known

There was the Swainson's in the thicket, the one I saw sing:
head thrown back, throat bubbling, high above the water.
There was the Wilson's in the thicket, the same thicket:
a little canary on a branch, head cocked, looking right at me.
There was the common yellowthroat along the road,
two days in a row—it was the same one, I think—
flitting around in the alder screens, its bright black mask

like a bandit's. I swear he knew me. Or by the ocean,
on the point, high above the only water I've seen you could
actually call aquamarine, and endlessly, all the way out
to the horizon, and up on the branch of an old-growth spruce
crowding the edge of the trail, big as a dog, a bald eagle,
so unmoving you thought at first it must be a statue of an eagle,
animatronic. But no, the clear yellow eyes blink, they click,

and the snowy white head turns on the flange of the neck,
very slowly, and the people are walking by and talking,
and then see it, and then stop, and point, and exclaim—and then,
on this sunny day above the sea, start passing back word of it,
person to person, down the trail, each one in turn handing on
what has been handed on to them—an eagle!—all the way back
to the curve where I am just now coming out into the open.

Plow

It could have been long ago: autumn in the trees,
a stubble field, a team of horses pulling a plow,
six enormous, farting roans, three on three—

we had come to watch a local farmer learning
how to horse plow—six enormous, milky roans,
stocky as rhinos, dragging the ancient discer

up and down the rows, snorting and champing,
digging at the turns like linebackers. It took them
so long to reach the far end, we had a chance to talk.

The farmer's wife. A man who shoed horses,
of all things. The air seemed to thin. A hill. An oak.
After a while, riding along for a furrow, you realize

you can hear beneath the chuffing and the groaning
the whisper of the plow as the earth falls back
from the blade. A gentle shushing, like waves.

River of Light

I thought I saw a river of light and two men in a boat,
working against the waves. But I was wrong.
It was just a log, caught in the current. Several birds.
Blinding sun. Andy's such a minimalist,
especially now that he's dead. So I fell asleep,
and when I woke, I was standing by the estuary,
down at the salty margin. And there, in the shallows,
was a heron. I watched him a long time. How he crossed
his skinny legs, one in front of the other, walking
sideways. How he kept pulling back his feathered head.
A little. A little more. But never struck. Not once.

Limited Edition

Limited Edition Tommy Drake loves a girl
with a studded tongue. She talks a lot, stud bobbing,
and Limited Edition, with his big shoulders and dark,
handsome face, sprawls in a chair and listens, half smiling.

Limited Edition is his stage name, of course.
He's a wrestler, for the WWE—I may have seen him
on TV, he says—and one day in Japan he loves the girl
with the studded tongue so much he can't breathe.

They've been arguing over the phone.
"I was asking and asking for her to speak. Still nothing.
I kept falling into despair. Then it happened.
I was rushed with every emotion I had all at once.
I was crying and laughing. I thought I would burst.
When she spoke, I didn't just hear her. I felt her.

Now my cheeks hurt from smiling all day.
The air smells different. When I look in the mirror
it's my reflection, but there's something else, too."

Limited Edition Tommy Drake is so full of joy
and wonder and love he understands everything,
God, Japan, the girl with the studded tongue.

"I can't tell you why I'm laughing," he says.

The John Day Fossil Beds: Clarno

The fossil of a leaf embossed
on the face of a rock
forty-four million years ago

is no more or less important
than the leaf that flutters
and waves outside the window.

The same dear little ribs.
The delicate nets of veins.
What remains of an ancient rhino

or a tiger or a tiny horse we find
familiar. A femur is still
a femur. A tooth is still a tooth.

The sign said every step we took
on that path among the stones
was worth thousands of years.

But doesn't every moment matter?

We are all afraid. We are all
running away from our loneliness.
But deep within our bodies we all

have hearts. We all have bones.
Beautiful, clean, white bones.
Like the treasure, buried in the field.

Chasm

Sometimes in the spring
there is a scent in the forest like mint.

Sometimes in the fall
there is a scent like tea, and the leaves
are the color of tea.

You descend into a deep chasm
thick with spruce and fir.
You are near the sea, and it is rainy
and wet, and you have to slap
through the salmonberry and fern
that hang over the path.
Before long you are soaked
clear through.

When you arrive at the bottom,
something seems to change.
The trees seem to pull back.
The birds begin to sing as if
you are approaching a ceremony.

But it is just a meadow, with a stream.

Clear water flowing
over smooth, gray stones.

Password

We're trying to get into Sue's computer,
but we can't because she's dead.
We don't know the password.

Just last week I was sitting across from her
at the Thai restaurant and I could have asked her
and she would have told me.

How little would have been required to cross
that threshold. Just a breath.
A movement of the tongue. A sound.

Walking in the forest today, down the road,
I found a long, smooth tail feather from a hawk,
gray and black and dirty white.

I brought it home with me.
I like how hard and stiff the quill is, like bone,
and yet how light, too, how hollow.

Holding it you think of flight—

though you also think of Dante
and Shakespeare and Keats,
dipping it in ink and starting to write.

II

My Atomic Energy Merit Badge

One dot orbiting another dot, in thread.
What could I have possibly done to earn it?
But I do remember Rick Morris
and driving up Slate Creek to see the stars.
It was the first time I ever looked
long enough to disappear. Oh my friends!
Where are you? The future is fast receding,
like the universe. It is speeding away.

Sliver

Grandpa Ted sits at a table in the room I always go to,
drinking gin from a mason jar. I never knew him—
he's been dead for fifty years—but somehow it doesn't seem
strange to be standing in the kitchen doorway, looking in.
He wears one of those white undershirts that don't have any
sleeves. He needs a shave. His eyes shine glassy and dark.

Once when my mother was a girl she was washing dishes
in a wooden sink and a sliver got stuck in her finger. It dug deep
into her flesh. But Grandpa's hands shook so hard when he tried
to hold the tweezers, he was so bleary and drunk, all he could do
was cry. Mom remembers this. How the tweezers shook above
her bloody finger. How the tears streamed down his stubbly chin.

Now he sits at a table in the room I always go to. It's morning
and he is drinking from a mason jar, skin sallow and damp. I think
how frail he is. But then he looks up. His eyes focus. He smiles.
He knows me, he knows everything about me, and he wants to say
something now, he wants to speak. So lifting up the jar with both hands,
the gin clear as water, he speaks to me in a voice stronger and deeper

than I thought it could be. "Take and drink," he says. "Take and drink."

Our Trip to Spokane at Thanksgiving

Sometimes I order exactly what I want.
A combination plate: chow mein,
fried rice, sweet-and-sour pork.
Outside, snow is falling on the dirty streets.
It's hard to say I love you
when you are the condition of my loving.
It's hard to really see you,
for you are my eyes.
Rolling fields. Along a river
a farm, with buildings and outbuildings.
A white fence. The cold, cold earth.
Not a tree in sight.

But My, Don't the Trees Seem Full

Opie accidentally killed a mother bird with his slingshot
and Andy made him take care of the baby birds, feeding
them worms with tweezers. At the end the chicks
were all grown up and Andy was standing on the porch
in his crisp, khaki uniform looking masculine and wise
the way he always did, sort of stern and compassionate
at the same time, and Opie realized he had to free the birds
from the cage he was keeping them in. He had to let them go.

You could see little Ron Howard's blond eyelashes
as he bravely lowered his head. He must have been five,
with those little boy shoulders all you want to do is squeeze.

That day on campus these big spaces had been opening up
before me. The halls were empty, nobody was around,
and this void kept yawning beneath my feet,
these long hours of silence when I felt like the speakers
in the Psalms when they talk about their spirits fainting
and the enemy crushing them to the ground. I didn't know
what to do except just sit there until it was time to go home.

So I was ready for the way the show ended, though
I knew of course that this wasn't really Mayberry and Andy
wasn't really Opie's father. But I was ready and grateful.

"The cage sure seems empty," Opie said, when the birds had flown.
"Yes, it does," Andy said. "But my, don't the trees seem full."

Then the camera pulled up and away and we were in
the treetops, and though there weren't any birds there really,
there was a soundtrack of some birds chirping and bubbling
and singing, and even after Andy put his arm around Opie
and they walked back into the house, I kept loving them
and thinking of my own sons when they were that age
and of my father, how sometimes I imagined him
in Andy's uniform, with that crease in the trousers—
how Andy never wore a gun, even when he should have.

Letting Go

Me on the easy end, four steps above,
barking my shins as we bumped it down,

Dad below, at the base, trying to do it all,
as always, sweat beading, tendons cording

with the effort to wrest that whole black piano
down that narrow, impossible passage

as I let it go—as I had to—

the weight of it slowly pulling away
like a great ship casting off for icy waters.

Like Honey

I could never hit the nail on the head,
but I loved the smell of lumber,
sharp and sweet and clean.

I loved the snugness of the gap
where we lay the plywood down,
the sense it made of shelter.

What I loved in the catalogs
wasn't really the Schwinns
but the sunny streets and leafy trees,

the happy boys and girls,
laughing by their ten-speeds.

I had heard the music of the spheres,
I had seen the planets spin—
one Sunday at the Garland,

gaping up at the screen—
the fetus floating
in an air lock, bright as an angel.

When we went to the Flamingo,
all I ate was the menu.
And it was good. It was very good.

It dripped down my throat like honey.

The Astronaut's Confession

The truth is I didn't get along with the other guys.
I admired them in a way, and they were nice enough,
in the simulators and on the missions. But secretly,
they bored me. Do you know, my commander turned
away when I poured wine on the moon? We had
just landed, and I said the Our Father and put the host
on my tongue. When I poured the little bottle of wine,
it flowed like a thick, red syrup—that slowly—but
the commander wasn't looking. I think he was nervous.
There was a pause, then we flipped more switches.

The LEM looked so small when I turned back
from a distance. I had driven the rover onto the rim
of a crater about five miles away, and from there
the lander looked like a spindly toy against
the Taurus Mountains. I was working then, just like
anyone else. I had my tools. I took sips of water.
My little house was waiting for me, down in the valley.
The hummocks and hills looked so soft and bright
I longed to lie down in their dust and never get up.

I left a lot of things on the moon. I left a gold ring.
I left my book. I left a picture of Mom and Dad
with me and Tim and Ted outside our church
at my Confirmation. I remember how red Mom's dress
looked against the gray, how suddenly I knew color
is a miracle. That's when I started writing in the dust,
like at a beach when you're marooned, but I was just
writing words. I wrote *God?* in big letters. I wrote
a *Yes* and a *No*. I wrote the name of my daughter.
I wrote a lot of words on the moon, words that no one
will ever know or see. They're all still up there.

Caesar's Last Breath

Some people just smile too fast for the camera.
They only look as if their eyes are closed,

because at just that moment they changed.
Like Johnny Carson. The way his head would

duck and his teeth would flash. Or my dad.
Man, was he quick. The way he could cross

a room. The way he'd slap me in the mouth
when I spoke out of turn. Like *that*.

Pard, he'd call me, *pal: be where you're at.*

But how, exactly?

Every Ides of March the scientists talk about
the air in his lungs when Caesar bled out.

That very second. On the steps of the portico,
after the stabbing. They say now and then

every person on the planet breathes in a molecule
he breathed out at the end, when he let it all go.

Or Shakespeare. Or Jesus.

What She Named Me

My mother named me Christ-Bearer,
Christopher, the one who bore the Boy
on his back, across the swollen river.

Though He was too heavy at first.
This was He who would bear the whole
weight of the world, and St. Christopher

staggered and shook beneath him,
up to his knees in the water. Finally,
exhausted, he had to turn around.

So the Boy planted Christopher's staff
in the ground, his shepherd's crook,
and the next day it had grown

into a lovely, green tree, thick
with flowers and fruit, and when he ate
of the fruit and breathed in the flowers,

Christopher took the Boy in his arms,
lifted him up onto his shoulders,
and strode out into the river, waves

breaking back from his thighs. Oh,
how the birds sang and the wood rang
when he set him down on the other side!

This is all just a myth, of course.
St. Christopher never really existed.
And my mother is dead,

a year ago Easter she died,
and none of us is sure who Dad is
without her, or who we are either.

Just today my brother wrote to say
that they'd driven up to Sullivan Lake,
he and Dad. It was peaceful as always,

not a soul around. Through the trunks
of the trees they could look out at the lake
the way I always remember. And they

talked and talked, my brother said,
story after story. All they did was talk.
All the way up and all the way back.

Knowing Something

When your mother dies
something happens in your body.

You are born on a mountain,
and where you grow up
there is a mountain,
and now there is a mountain, too,
beyond it, the sea.

A summer storm. Hunched,
you run across a bridge
made of girders.

The river pounding
and booming.

Bing Crosby's Dorm

The dorm where I lived was Bing Crosby's dorm
years before, until he tried to lower a piano
from a fourth-floor window. When the rope snapped,
they expelled him. My room was on the first floor
across from a courtyard with a metal statue of Jesus.
At night snow would fall on the face of the Lord,
and the radiator would hiss and pop, and I'd put
Rachmaninoff on the stereo Mom gave me
for Christmas. Lying in the warmth and the light,
listening to the horns and strings and those huge, dark
chords swelling and building, I'd feel all the things
I couldn't put into words, sadness and sweetness
and a strange, joyous grief. Bing was just a crooner.
He lilted. All he sang in the movies were serenades.
When he came in the spring, for the last time, signing
autographs on the steps of the library they'd named
for him, I kept walking. I had better things to do.
And then he died. Just a few weeks later. He died
on the eighteenth hole—in Spain, I think—his friends
all around him. Brilliant grass. Maybe the sun
was shining. Maybe they could look out on the sea.
I think we should all forgive our younger selves.
Our earnestness. Our self-regard. But I really wish
I'd stopped and joined the others on the steps that day.
I wish I'd taken the chance to shake his hand
and look into those cold, blue eyes. To see if he knew.

I Tell Mr. Rogers My Dog Died

I should have written before, when
you were still alive and I was really a boy.
I always admired how slow you were,
and brave, how you never turned away.
Christmas our dog died, a border collie,
sweet faced. His name was Max.
We buried him on the hill, and every time
I walk past the little cross we put up,
I ache to be with him again—not much,
I admit, but every time. Now it's April,
and wild iris are blooming by his grave,
and a silence opens up the way it used to
on your show when you were just being
in the room. You'd be sitting in a chair,
before the next thing, and you'd let
the camera show your face going
empty and still the way every face
really is. That's what I admired.

Stephen Hawking Experiences Weightlessness

Copernicus, walking in a field and looking at stars,
fell down a well. Or was it Kepler?
Neither could tell his ass from a hole in the ground,
as my father once said of me, and he should know.
He never takes a major arterial, only side streets—
he's always zigging and zagging his way home.
Look at Stephen Hawking, the famous physicist.
The other day he went up in the Vomit Comet,
describing parabolas above the Cape.
"Space, here I come!" he is reported to have said.
The only muscle he can move is in his cheek,
but for seconds at a time, again and again, he flew
through the air like a diver, dipping and gliding.
"It was amazing," he said. "I could have gone on and on."
As someday, I believe, we will.

Fold

What I like about dreams are the verbs.
Flying. Running down a corridor.
I am always a character.
Growing up it was different:
we never did anything. You could tell
just walking into the house
what kind of mood she was in,
whether life that day had any meaning.
Later, when I would drive back
through the desert to see her,
it was like moving toward a giant
sheet of paper full of paragraphs
I was getting ready to read aloud.
It hung in the sky over the Palouse.
I didn't even know.
How the bare land would dip and fold.

Three Theories of the Spine

Jacob slipped a disc wrestling by the river. The L5, probably,
pain and spasms down the left leg, numbness in the foot.
That's why he limped away at dawn (from the hip, Genesis says).
All night it was dark and the man was wily, and he kept throwing
Jacob down, over and over, and he wouldn't give his name,
wouldn't budge, but Jacob decided he was an angel, that he was
from God—that he *was* God—and that must have helped a lot
during his long recovery. Six to eight weeks, the doctor says.

꩜

My massage therapist claims that when pain leaves a leg,
the leg is lighter. She can feel it the next time in her hands
(she says), how it almost floats, is almost buoyant. She's holding
my foot as she says this, kneading the sole. Maybe that's why
Dante kept getting lighter and lighter on the way up Purgatory
as first one sin, then another, was burned away, Pride and Anger
and all the rest, until finally at the top, in the Earthly Paradise,
he and Beatrice just flew into space. He was healing.

꩜

Or consider this, my masseuse says. (Her name is Piper,
and she used to be an engineer.) In the old days people noticed
when they burned a body that only one bone was left, too thick
to burn, part of the pelvis, the posterior wall, and so they called it
the sacrum. It was sacred. It remained. And that's where the spirit
coils, you know, at the fulcrum, ready and waiting. All the spine
has to do is straighten out enough for the soul to reach the skull,
which is also pretty thick. It snaps up, like a whip.

Brothers

We were brothers.
When we climbed the mountain
we thought the mountain cared.

Blue skies. Bright gulfs of air.
Across from us, a greater, snowy peak.
Then, as we struck camp,

screaming down the valley,
flat gunmetal gray, wings brutal as knives,
a bristling Air Force F-16,

banking so close to where we were
on the mountain, for a moment we could see
through the plexiglas the head of the pilot.

The dark helmet.
The glistening mask.

The Story of My Career

In the first part of my career I traveled around
and let myself be swallowed by dragons. Every
village had one, a big one or a medium-sized one,
encrusted with spikes and scales. Once inside
I slit open the belly with a small rapier I made
especially for this purpose, then slid out
with the viscera and the fluids. It was like being
born again, except that my mother always died.

In the next stage I became a hermit and lived
in a cave, where for a while a serpent lived, too,
a long, green, muscled snake. It coiled beside me
as I prayed or slithered into bed with me at night.
But I refused to be driven away. I even dared it
to bite me. Finally, after several long years,
it rushed out into the open, hissing furiously,
and set the brush ablaze with the sparks that flew
from its flickering tongue. Then the rain came

and put out the fire. The air finally cleared.
Now I am alone all day, thinking and praying,
and in the evening I come out to watch the sun
go down. I sit on a hill above the sea and wait.
It takes about an hour. The thing I never knew
about sunsets is that most of them are pretty
disappointing. There are too many clouds
or the sun just drops away. But sometimes
they're spectacular. The clouds darken and glow
and the light shoots out everywhere, salmons
and oranges and pinks, great shafts of gold.
It's like the beginning of bombs going off.

Crushing Rocks

Once I was a rock crusher for the U.S. Bureau of Mines,
grinding sacks of granite into samples fine as flour.
The Pulverizer, the Shaker, the Sanding Plates,
first rubble, then gravel, then powder flecked with gold,
sifted into sandwich bags and filed away on trays,
one bulging, jagged sack after another, fifty, sixty pounds
of glittering ore, into the hoppers and out the chutes,
pebbled and pummeled by degrees, machine by machine.
This was our vocation, and it can be again. The whir
and the whine, the rise and the fall, hour after hour, day
after day. The steady, soothing drone. The sun on the wall
where we took our breaks—outside, in the parking lot,
in the silence and the air, pushing up our dusty masks
and gladly leaning back—our minds become so blank,
our spirits so attuned, we could nap once in the morning
and once in the afternoon. Ten minutes. Exactly.

strophic
stichic

Hank Asks about Angels

Politely, with all apparent innocence and curiosity,
Hank has come to ask about angels. As if I might
really know the answer. As if anyone would.

Late afternoon, November, my office warm and bright.
When I look out the window into the darkness,
all I see is my own reflection.

Hank purses his young man's lips, pushes back
his young man's hair. His hands are small.

Professorial, I put up my feet and stall: choirs, Hank,
choirs, at least in Dante, everyone flying back and forth
and singing, though only metaphor, of course, only image,
because all we really know is joy, and only now and then.
Or forests, Hank. Think forests, the deep trees and great trunks.
We walk and walk in fragrance and shadow, or I have at least,
I have—haven't you? Surely in your life, even in the malls
and before the screen, you have felt the brush of what seems
like wings? What has swept past you, lifted up? What rush of air?

His eyes are brown, and soft, and small. I think of him
as a baby. I think of going home. I think of the bare trees
outside and the darkness, maybe stars.

Or the Aquarium. Yes. The Oregon Coast Aquarium.
I think of that morning by the huge window cut
into the rock where the seals and the sea lions glide past
goofy and blissful in the murk and the salt and the joyous
buoyant water of the sea like ridiculous soft missiles,
like dirigibles, one of them—look at him!—one of them
upside down, tiny flippers tight against his blubbery body,
eyes closed, a whiskery smirk on his silly, wizened face,
improbable as Dr. Seuss. Oh, how they squeeze and glide
round that endless tank, aimed and unerring and true,
nonchalant, purling and flipping among the pillars
with what marvelous virtuosity, entirely weightless
and free, veering so close you think they must collide,
then curving apart and flying away, up and around
that endless, luminous tank like skaters, like clowns.

Maybe it's like that, Hank. Maybe it's like that.

Yes, he says, with a slight nod. OK.
But what about *the angels*? What about *the Bible*?

I pause and nod, too. I look at him again.

But I'm thinking of summer, in Spokane. I'm thinking
of that afternoon in the garden at Manito Park, overwhelmed
by the fragrance of roses, hundreds of roses, Patience and Peace
and Double Delight, scarlet and lavender and gold. The lawn
is green and smooth. The sun shines down, the bright sun
of my youth, through ponderosa. My son and daughter
move among the flowers, laughing. Oh Hank, I wish I could
explain how happy I felt among the rows, among the carefully
tended legions and ranks of those marvelous soft flowers,
or later, in the greenhouse, among the bamboo and the lilies
and the honeysuckle, shelf by shelf and row by row. We can
smell the dampness and the earth of the pots and the greenness.
A little stream runs beneath a bridge, and we stroll within the dome,
under glass, in the warm, moist air, and everywhere we look
the green leaves and the flowers open out and drop and reach
in all profusion and abundance and indifference, overflowing
their labels and their pots—indifference, you understand:
mindless green joy and push and patience—

Hank is arranging his books now, reaching for his coat.
He has been sitting erect, attentive, but he is smiling now,
abstractly, zipping up his backpack—

like the time in North Carolina, years ago, when my children
were babies, in the atrium of a zoo. Was it Raleigh?—a milky,
translucent, geodesic dome, multifaceted on the outside, and inside,
among the palms and the ferns, the birds hiding and singing
and sweeping down in their white capes and yellow fans and flaming
crowns, feathers spread like sails, like enormous, great balloons.
Some had beaks like nutcrackers, others like wedges of melon.
Some sang inside the soft darkness of the leaves, out of sight,
though sometimes, if you stopped and waited, perfectly still,
they'd brush past you with their wings. I can't help thinking
it was black outside, it was dark, but we were walking within
the jewel, we were enclosed, breathing in the air and the steam,
and the birds were singing and flying all around us,
toucans and cuckoos and parrots, the scarlet ibis, the nightingale,
and we walked and walked and never came to the end,
never touched the glass of the outer wall. We could have
been anywhere. We could have been in space.

III

The Thing about Hell

The thing about Hell
is that the deeper you go
the narrower it gets
until finally you're standing
in the Center for the Humanities.
Everyone is crowding
the narrow little rooms
and you can't move.

You're stuck.

That night, blessedly,
it starts to rain.
And it rains so hard
you wake up
and open a window
so you can listen
to the abundance of rain
and the generosity of rain.

The precision of rain:
every leaf.

Stardust

Once by a pond I watched cedar waxwings
swoop and stall, snatching insects. I'd never seen

so many before in one place. Their dark masks.
Their yellow-dipped tails. Later, evening.

Once in a meadow I lost my silver rosary.
A small one with a clasp, the kind a girl might wear.

But it wasn't hard to find, the way it glittered
later in the grass, like a string of tiny pearls.

Once at a funeral an old man slowly rose
and belted out "Stardust." Teary eyed. Quavering.

Oh memories of love! The purple dust of twilight
steals across the meadows of our hearts!

I wasn't expecting this. But after a while
I realized how beautiful life is, and sad.

Nothing is ever lost.
It's always just somewhere else.

In Town

I never knew how much I like clocks
until I happened to walk into a clockmaker's shop
and it was a festival of clocks and a cathedral of clocks
and there were a hundred thousand tiny, golden gears
turning a hundred thousand tiny, golden wheels.

I also like the sound of the word *breakfast*
and the idea of the word *breakfast*. I like the sound
of the word *lunch* and the idea of the word *lunch*.
I like the clink of the spoon as it taps the cup.
I like the clattering of plates and the gathering of voices
and the air that rises in the warm, fragrant rooms.

Later I walk along the river. Bright sun. Couples.
Linden trees. The river is always moving,
it's always flowing, wide and wrinkly and brown.
But every time I've looked, it's always been there.

Seven More Parables of the Kingdom

The Kingdom of Heaven is like the room in your dream
and outside is a lake so blue and cold you know
something big is about to happen. Then you wake up
and have your coffee and don't think about the dream again.

⟡

The Kingdom of Heaven is like writing fast and not leaving
anything out and the same idea that always forms
starts to form again. You know it's just an idea, you know
you're just floating on the surface of Reason, but underneath
the sentences you feel something big pushing up from the dark.

⟡

The Kingdom of Heaven is like when you're walking on the docks
and your best friend from high school sees you a hundred yards away
and even after all these years knows it's you. You have the same walk,
he says. You lean the same way. All this time this man was alive
and you were, too, and you didn't think about each other for decades,
and now he takes you in his boat to the other side of the lake
and his wife is making jello and the cabin is full of pots and pans
and dog-eared books he has read and reread just like you.
All those cabins in the trees! All those roads winding out to highways
and cities you've never been to, with offices and neighborhoods
and parks where kids are throwing footballs.

⟡

The Kingdom of Heaven is like the spine, which you also never think of.
Most of the time you don't even know you have one, until one day
the doctor explains how discs darken as you get further down
what for all the world looks like a lobster tail. Segmented. Curving left.

And though the evidence is blurry and gray, like those fuzzy photographs
of UFOs that always turn out to be dishes, suddenly you know without
    a doubt
this one is true. This is what you carry, this slippery fulcrum, this meaty
    device.

⁂

Walking up the little valley. Morning. Heavy dew.
Suddenly a field of spiders, a field of webs,
every thistle strung like a racket.

⁂

The Kingdom of Heaven is like the ecology of your yard. All these animals
are scurrying around and building nests and entering into all these
    conflicts
and alliances just like in a Walt Disney movie or a book by E. B. White.
And you never see them, usually, maybe a squirrel now and then, a bird,
but you never give them a moment's thought, never think about them
    at all,
until one morning you walk out the door to get the paper and nearly step
on a headless mouse, eviscerated, heart and lungs spilling from the breast.
Another gift from the cats, another sign of their prowess.

⁂

Those shiny viscera on the welcome mat.
Those intricate systems, inside out.
That dark red heart, like a coat of arms.

Wisdom

Wisdom comes forth from the mouth of God
  and covers the earth like mist, says Sirach.

You can see it now, hanging in the spruce
  and the hemlock above Nestucca Bay.

Wisdom comes forth from the mouth of God
  and pours on the earth like hard, winter rain.

It runs in the gutters and swells the streams,
  flooding the fields along the Little Nestucca.

Wisdom comes forth from the mouth of God
  and breaks through the trees like sun. It steams

the back of the doe that nibbles in the yard.
  You have been out walking, looking for God.

She doesn't startle. She lifts her head and shows you
  her large, empty eyes, her chin going round and round,

and for the first time in your life you can hear her
  ruminating, loud and clear as a kid eating cornflakes.

Here Is the Man Who Does This

One morning I woke up with the ability to see myself.
It was as if I were in an operating room,
looking down on my body,
except I wasn't dying. I was just brushing my teeth
and having my thoughts.
I was both good and bad. Happy and sad.
I was ebbing and flowing like always,
but I was also the person who always ebbs and flows.
I kept thinking, here is the man who does this.
Worries. Holds on. Lets go. Doubts. Believes.
And that was fine with me. I liked this person
well enough. He qualified as a person.
Outside, heavy rain. Gusty winds. The first big storm.

Rose

It's winter now, and cold, and this morning
by the confluence of two rivers
I stood and prayed the rosary, stamping and blowing.
I never know what good this does,
but afterward I felt a little better. A little clearer.
Mist was rising from the surface of the water,
and the sun was coming out,
and there seemed to be several stories
of light and mist and air, then a range of hills
I hadn't known was there.
Every vocation is a mystery.
Even the smoke that poured from the factory
was thick and bright. A beautiful rose.

Piper's Dad

An old man is dying in a dark, fetid room.
His daughter is with him, in her kindness, praying
and holding his hand, though he was a harsh

and bitter man all his life and abused her
and abused his wife. He had been in combat
in a war and maybe that was it, but now

he is dying in a dark, fetid room and he is rigid
in his narrow, little bed, shaking, hands clenched,
and his daughter is with him. When I come

to read the Psalms to him, he seems to recognize
the rhythm of the words and how one line
is parallel to the next, and this seems to soothe him

for a while. He doesn't shake as much.
His eyes stop darting back and forth beneath
the stony lids. And later, after I leave, he opens

his eyes. He seems to focus for a moment.
He seems to look through the darkness
at his daughter, and he says two words to her,

in a faint, croaking voice: *You bitch.*
Who knows what this man was thinking
or what he was seeing. Maybe he wasn't talking

to his daughter, maybe he was talking to Death,
but this is what he says, *You bitch,*
and this is what his daughter does. She rises

from that chair, and she leans over that bed,
and she whispers in her father's ear:
Daddy, I love you. And that night, he dies.

Love is a great emptying out and losing.
Love is a rising from a chair. It is a leaning
over a bed. It is a whisper in a room and a word

in a room. The last thing this man
ever said was ugly and vulgar and mean.
But this wasn't the last thing he ever heard.

The Anthropologist Within

Like all emotions, anger doesn't understand time.
Some nights the moon shines so bright you can even read in the yard.
Stars. Leaves. My Polartec, bristling with seeds.
The dead outnumber the living fourteen to one,
and half of them are babies. Let's say, eighty-five billion to five-point-nine.
But there are many ways to understand the hermeneutics of generosity.
Unwilling to keep my soul's substance for You, I take it for myself.
And wishing to possess myself without You, I lose both You and myself.
My heart turns to stone. My tear ducts run dry.
What then? Into the fields I go to read the Holy Book.
I set down my thoughts, and suddenly Rebecca comes running toward me,
and with her, light, which is Your grace, good Jesus.
"Honey," she says, "are you incapable of complexity?"

Everything That Rises Must Converge

To Flannery O'Connor, who died
in the summer, 1964,
this might have seemed like the far future.

She might have imagined
we'd have flying cars by now
or great cities on the moon. Or maybe not.

In the picture on the back of the book
of her letters, she is balancing
on two aluminum crutches, in a dark dress

and pearls, looking down at a peacock.
This is on her mama's farm,
in Georgia, at the top of some brick steps.

Old-lady glasses, though she was just
thirty-nine. A mousey bob,
though her friends used to speak

of her clear, rosy skin and beautiful eyes.
The white frame of the screen door
behind her is scratched and peeling.

We are so different. "I've never been
anywhere but sick," she wrote.
She believed the Church was infallible.

She would have fixed me with a stare.
She would have soon discovered
the weakness that makes me who I really am.

But it is late spring now and warm.
The moon is coming up at the top of our drive,
above the trees. And passing the door

on the way to bed, book in hand, I pause
on an impulse and slip outside, walking up
to where the moonlight floods the road.

"Remember these are mysteries," she said.
"A God you could understand would be less
than yourself." And I find that I have carried her

with me, I am holding her in my arms,
here, in the next century, in the brilliant night.

Morning with the Dying Man

I broke bread with the dying man
and slept in the dying man's house
and in the morning before the sun rose
sat with him at table and drank the coffee
he had made, chatting about ordinary things.
At first we were surrounded by darkness.
The breakfast lights shone and the window
looking out to the sea and the storms
became a mirror in which all we could see
was ourselves, our cups, our faces.
But the surf was booming in the distance.
We could hear it. And gradually the light
seeped back and we could see the edges
of trees and the waves cresting beyond
the mouth of the river, just as we knew
we would. The wide sea. The sky.
It was always there, the dying man said.
It's the world, the enormous world.

Another Story about Sue

Sue was loud and brash. Big. Always joking.
A year after she died, some people were cleaning out
a closet at church and came across a few envelopes,

addressed and sealed. They'd been misplaced
after a retreat. The idea was to write down what you
most needed in your life, what you were praying for,

put it in an envelope, and address it to yourself.
The retreat leader would mail it to you later, after you'd
forgotten about it. The insight you'd had. The hope.

Sue had been at that retreat, and one of those lost letters
was hers. So they opened it. They weren't sure they
should, but they did. It seemed right. And what they found

inside was a single word, in large letters. *Silence.*

Who would have guessed? No one was going to see this.
This was you being honest with yourself. And what Sue
wanted, deep down, what she longed for, was silence.

And now she has it. It has been given to her.

Why I Like the Tomb

It's peaceful, like the house where I grew up,
with the warm stone walls and the earth floor
I swept clean every day with straw.

Outside, the cattle were lowing
and sometimes looking in with enormous eyes
like small, brown planets.

I don't know what I was afraid of.

      ❧

Beyond the walls of the cave there is a garden.
The sun rises and sets and rises again.
Warblers fret in the brittle trees.
Sometimes I think I even hear the rustling
of the snake on its marvelous, oily scales!

      ❧

The darkness. The blessed darkness.
Like the darkness of the garden
before they came with their torches,
the clamoring crowds and the soldiers
in their leather, jeering, too.

This darkness is what was made for us
and to this we all return.

The dry leaves of the olive trees.
The night breeze.

How the rabbit and the mouse
waited in the shadows,
perfectly still, watching us
with eyes like bright, black buttons.

Pip

If there were an earthquake and you were on the moon
looking down, you wouldn't see any movement at all.
Even with a big one. No crumbling. No cracking.

The earth would seem to just hang there in space,
seas a deep blue, clouds creamy white. And it's good
to look at life like this sometimes, from a distance,

because it humbles us and exalts us and it makes us aware
of how fragile life is and interconnected, the way it did
the astronauts, gazing homeward through their hatches.

But it's good, too, to zoom in and to keep on zooming,
from high up all the way down to the very pixel you're in,
to the living room and to the couch in the living room

and to the little dog sleeping on top of the back cushions
of the couch, his head and his front paws draped over
your shoulder in such a way that one day during Holy Week,

when in the scene from the Last Supper in the gospel
that morning the Beloved Disciple leans back in his love
and his sadness and his grief against the chest of Our Lord,

your left ear is pressed against the chest of that little dog,
and you hear through the layers of his fur and the muscle
and the bone the steady beating of his little doggy heart.

You sit there a long time. You hold very still.

The Earth, of Course

At the ashram Paul kept writing songs.
He couldn't help it. "Talk to me!"
the Maharishi cried, plaintively, but
it was too late. Paul was driving away.

In the gorge the river boiled. Shadows
fell on even the highest mountains.

When it finally left the solar system,
billions of miles out, they turned
the probe around: pale bands of light,
like a fabric, sage and cream and rose.

The earth, of course, a speck. A dot.

Astronomically speaking,
we are insignificant.

But astronomically speaking,
we are the astronomers.

Whatever Else, the Blessed Days

When the morning star hangs in the oak tree,
   I rejoice and am glad, oh Lord,
though just a little, I have to admit,
   as it's early, and I am groggy, and the star

wavers and blurs as if through water,
   and my seeing of it depends, of course,
on the orbit and tilt of two planets
   I am absolutely sure know me not,

spinning in space inconceivably
   far apart, without intelligence or regard.
Still, some branches of the oak *do* bend,
   horizontally, like the edges around

the spaces where puzzle pieces go,
   and for the moment the star *does* glow,
right in the middle of the wavy frame
   the branches make, soft and beautiful,

it seems to me, from my angle, and the air
   is soft, too, and cool, for the first time
all this summer long. Every morning
   the sky darkens more and more.

My God, the first leaves of the maple
    are even starting to turn! And though I will
have forgotten this by midday, or sooner—
    by my second cup of coffee—

what thrills in me for just a moment
    is the sure and certain knowledge
that whatever else, the blessed days
    are growing shorter.

My Trip through the Afterlife

One of my favorite parts was when Beatrice
stopped bawling me out and we shot into heaven.
I saw the Earthly Paradise recede,

the meadows and trees, and when I looked up
I understood space isn't empty really but like water,
silver, then red, then gold, band after band.

I loved being weightless. My body shot higher
and higher and I was bathed in light
and Beatrice knew everything I was thinking.

People think heaven is boring but it's not.
Music pours from the Empyrean.
Mr. Rogers is there, in his sweater. Lincoln.

Grandma Gottwig dances in a circle of saints,
hair just as blue as ever. Behind her
the Big Bang is happening again, matter is flying

everywhere, and she laughs and laughs.

We Will Go Rejoicing

How many therapists does it take to change a lightbulb?
One.
But the lightbulb has to really want to change.
Be not afraid. Have no anxiety at all.
There's a bend in the road on the way to Colville.
Beyond it lies the treasured valley.
A velvet moose lifts a velvet hoof. Cups clatter.
This is no illusion, believe me.
Dad always said he'd walk up the mountain, but I really have.
To get to the other side.

What Trees Do

Every morning I am given all this wisdom,
and every afternoon I throw it all away.

I can't pray. I can only walk:
the forest is my audience.

There is a hill behind me, it has always been
behind me, and it has been given to me to climb,

especially in the summer and in the morning
when it is cool and soft and I can tell the trees

all know and love me.
If I were to die at the top, overlooking

the valley, if my body were to drop,
the trees wouldn't move.

They would never leave me.
They would just keep rising.

Notes

The epigraph is from Richard Hugo's *Triggering Town*.

The word *alb* in "A Summer Day" (p. 4) refers to the white robe that priests and deacons wear when participating in a liturgy. The line of scripture I quote, the basis of the final blessing in the Catholic graveside service, is Philippians 4:7.

"Move Over, Darling" (p. 8) is the title of the Doris Day movie I talk about in the poem.

The opening stanza of "People of Galilee" (p. 12) is a paraphrase of Acts 1:11. The joke in the second stanza is from a Woody Allen essay, "My Speech to the Graduates."

The title and the first few images of "The Watchful Tree" (p. 14) are adapted from the *New Jerusalem Bible*'s translation of Jeremiah 1:11, 1:13, and 18:1–4.

"Sacristan" (p. 16) refers to the person in charge of a church's sacred vessels and vestments. Since Vatican II, this is usually a layperson. A "pyx" is a container, often made of a precious metal, used for bringing Communion to the sick.

The last line of "Foundation" (p. 18) is a paraphrase of Isaiah 30:21.

The line about eating the menu in "Like Honey" (p. 35) is a paraphrase of a remark by Joseph Campbell in *The Power of Myth*, a book based on his conversations with Bill Moyers in the PBS series. The image of the menu "dripping down my throat like honey" echoes Ezekiel 3:1–3.

In "The Astronaut's Confession" (p. 36) I borrow details from the lives of Apollo astronauts Buzz Aldrin (*Apollo 11*), Gene Cernan (*Apollo 17*), and Charlie Duke (*Apollo 16*) as reported by Andrew Chaikin in *A Man on the Moon: The Voyages of the Apollo Astronauts*.

The story I tell in the first part of "Bing Crosby's Dorm" (p. 42) is apocryphal. Bing did go to Gonzaga University, where later I was also a student, but he wasn't expelled. He dropped out. He didn't live on campus. And what he lowered from a window—of the main administration building—wasn't a piano but a set of drums. But it is true that Bing died on a golf course in Spain in 1977 as he was walking off the eighteenth green. According to Gary Giddins in *Bing Crosby: A Pocketful of Dreams*, the last thing he ever said was, "That was a great game of golf, fellas." Then he collapsed with a massive heart attack and died.

The images in the first stanza of "The Story of My Career" (p. 48) are based on the legend of a fourth-century saint, Margaret of Antioch. I took the details in the second stanza from the legend of another saint—I know I read this somewhere—but for the life of me I can't seem to find the original source.

"Seven More Parables of the Kingdom" (p. 60) alludes to the seven parables in the thirteenth chapter of Matthew.

The title of "The Anthropologist Within" (p. 67) and the phrase "the hermeneutics of generosity" are from Paul Farmer, MD, as quoted by Tracy Kidder in his book about Farmer, *Mountains Beyond Mountains*. The question in the last line is a question that Dr. Farmer was asked by a woman he encountered in Haiti. The lines about the soul in the second half of the poem are paraphrases of two passages from Basil Pennington's edition of the selected writings of a twelfth-century Scottish monk, Aelred of Rievaulx.

The first stanza of "The Earth, of Course" (p. 76) is based on an episode in the life of Paul McCartney. The joke at the end of the poem is from a friend of mine, Eric Hill, who attributes it to his father.

The statistics in "The Old Woman and the Stars" (p. 17) and "The Anthropologist Within" (p. 67) are from Annie Dillard's *For the Time Being*.

The occasional numbers, facts, and biographical details in other poems come from various other sources.

Colophon

The titles are composed in Bernhard Modern,
a classic serif font designed in 1937 by Lucian Bernhard.
The text is set in Goudy Old Style,
designed in 1915 by Frederic W. Goudy.

Typesetting and layout by ImPrint Services,
Corvallis, Oregon.